I'm Reading About

GEORGIA

The Peach State!

GALLOPADE

by Carole Marsh

Printed and Manufactured in Peachtree City, GA., USA
www.gallopade.com

Book design: John Hanson
Editorial manager: Janice Baker

Georgia is a great state.
It is one of a kind.

What makes Georgia special?
Let's read about it
and see!

NATIVE AMERICANS

Who lived in Georgia first?

Native Americans did!

They moved around to find food.
They hunted in Georgia's woods.
They fished in Georgia's rivers.
They gathered fruits and seeds and nuts.

EXPLORERS

The first explorers came to Georgia in 1540.
They came from the country of Spain.

Hernando de Soto was their leader.
He and his men were looking for cities of gold!

SETTLEMENT

A man named James Oglethorpe
came from England to America.
He started the first settlement in Georgia.
He named it Savannah.

Georgia was one of
the original 13 colonies.

Savannah

STATEHOOD

Georgia was the fourth state
to join the United States of America!

Isn't it great,
to be a state!
I bet Georgia
could hardly wait!

Georgia became a state in 1788.

Georgia
The 4th State
Here we are!

FLAG

I am the state flag.
I was adopted in 2003.

What colors am I?
Red. White. Blue. Gold.

Count my stars.
Count my stripes.

Look at me.
What else do you see?

CONSTITUTION
WIS DOM
JUSTICE
MODER ATION
IN GOD WE TRUST

CAPITAL

Say hello to Atlanta:
the capital city of Georgia!

There is an important building in Atlanta.
It is the State Capitol.
Georgia laws are made there!

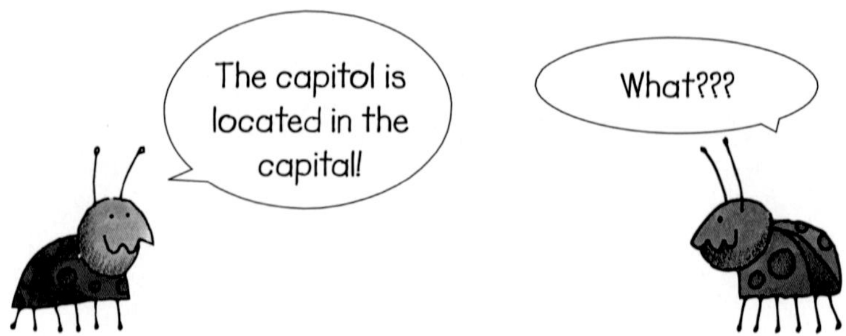

Capitol

Capital

SEAL

I am a seal,
but I am not the State Seal.
If I were, I would be very important.
I would be stamped on many official papers.
(Ouch, that might hurt!)

STATE OF GEORGIA
CONSTITUTION
WIS DOM
JUSTICE
MODER ATION
1776
Now, that's official!

NICKNAME

State nicknames are fun!
State nicknames are great!
They share fun facts
about each state!

Georgia's nickname is "The Peach State."

Georgia peaches sure are popular!

The Peach State

BORDERS

Look at Georgia.
Georgia is in a region called "the South."

Georgia borders five other states.
Find them on the map!

Georgia was named for King George II of England.

Borders

NORTH CAROLINA
TENNESSEE
SOUTH CAROLINA
GEORGIA
ALABAMA
ATLANTIC OCEAN
FLORIDA
Howdy, neighbors!

PRESIDENT

Jimmy Carter was the 39th President
of the United States of America.
He was born in Georgia!

Jimmy Carter grew up in a town called Plains.
His dad was a peanut farmer.
Jimmy ate lots of peanuts growing up!

Jimmy Carter

PEOPLE

Many famous people

Mary Musgrove

Creek Indian who helped James Oglethorpe

John Ross

Chief of the Cherokee nation

Juliette Gordon Low

Founded the Girl Scouts of the United States of America

call our state home!

Margaret Mitchell
Author of the famous novel *Gone With the Wind*

Jackie Robinson
First African American player in Major League Baseball

Martin Luther King, Jr.
Leader of the Civil Rights Movement

Brown Thrasher

I am the state bird, and I fly
over Georgia, proud and high.

As I fly, up in the sky,
I flap my wings to tell you "Hi!"

The Georgia state bird is the Brown Thrasher.

BIRD

Cherokee Rose

FLOWER

I am the Cherokee Rose.
I am the state flower.

I grow where it's warm and sunny.
I climb over shrubs and walls.
I help make Georgia beautiful!

Look at me! Smell me!
But don't touch my sharp thorns!

Live Oak

TREE

I am a Live Oak—I'm the state tree.
Along the coast is where to find me.

My roots run deep, they keep me strong.
My leaves stay green, all year long.

I stand up straight, big and tall.
Don't climb too high—it would hurt to fall!

Honeybee

INSECT

I am the Honeybee.
I am the state insect.

I might sting you if you bother me,
But really, I am your friend.

I carry pollen from flower to flower.
I make honey.
I help Georgia crops grow.

BZZZZZZZZZZZZ!

Atlantic Ocean

BEACHES

Let's go to the beach!

We can swim in the waves.
We can play in the sand.

We can build a big castle
where water meets land.

Georgia's barrier islands are home to many animals:

Sea Turtles **Wild Ponies** **Birds** **Crabs** **Dolphins** **and More!**

Blue Ridge Mountains

MOUNTAINS

Georgia's Blue Ridge Mountains
are the place to be.
Hiking, fishing, camping—
fun for you and me.

If you were to climb
to the top of a tree,
you could see clear to Tennessee!

Okefenokee Swamp

SWAMPS

The Okefenokee Swamp is the largest swamp in North America!
It is in south Georgia.

This habitat is home to many animals:

Birds Deer Snakes Frogs Alligators and More!

More than 15,000 alligators live in the Okefenokee Swamp!

Stone Mountain

LANDMARK

Stone Mountain is a giant rock!
It is made of granite.
It rises above ground like a mountain.
That's how it got its name!

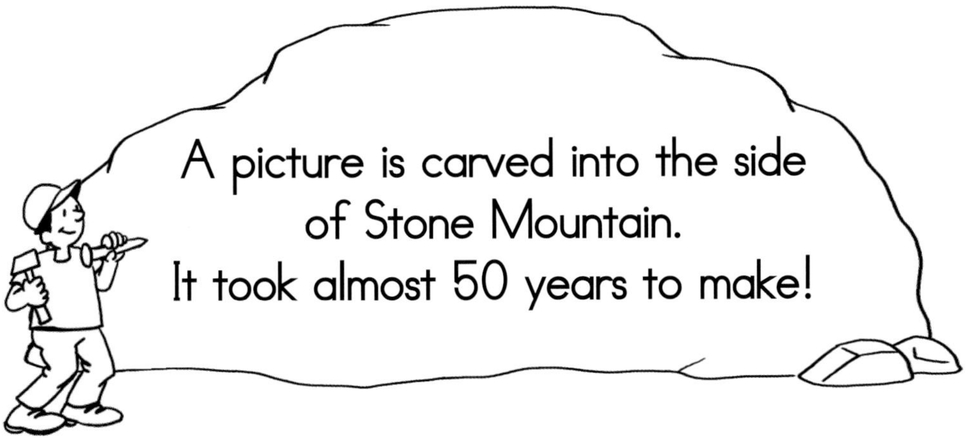

A picture is carved into the side
of Stone Mountain.
It took almost 50 years to make!

Georgia Crops

Georgia has many farms.
Why?
Because Georgia has good soil and a warm climate!

Georgia is known for the "three P's":

Peanuts **Peaches** **Pecans**

Sports in Georgia

SPORTS

Baseball! Basketball! Football!
Georgia has it all.

Whether you like to watch or play,
You are sure to have a ball!

Braves **Falcons** **Hawks**

Yellow Jackets

Bulldogs

& More!

Georgia: Home of Coca-Cola

CLAIM TO FAME

Coca-Cola was invented in Georgia!
A pharmacist from Atlanta
created the drink in 1886.
His name was John Pemberton.

The first servings of Coca-Cola sold for 5 cents per glass!

GLOSSARY

climate: weather conditions in an area over a long period of time

colony: a settlement ruled by another country

elect: to choose someone by voting

habitat: a place where plants or animals naturally live

laws: rules made by the government

pharmacist: a person who prepares and sells medicines

pollen: a yellow powder that helps plants make new plants

region: an area that has similar characteristics

settlement: the first community in an area

swamp: a low area of land that is often partly covered with water